D1555965

GRIEF,
LOVE,
AND OTHER
LIGHT
TOPICS

GRIEF, LOVE, AND OTHER LIGHT TOPICS

ROY G FAULKNER

LitPrime
"Your story is our priority"

LitPrime Solutions
21250 Hawthorne Blvd
Suite 500, Torrance, CA 90503
www.litprime.com
Phone: 1 (209) 788-3500

© 2020 Roy Faulkner. All rights reserved.

No part of this book may be reproduced, stored in a retrieval system, or transmitted by any means without the written permission of the author.

Published by LitPrime Solutions   11/20/2020

ISBN: 978-1-953397-33-1(sc)
ISBN: 978-1-953397-34-8(e)

Any people depicted in stock imagery provided by iStock are models, and such images are being used for illustrative purposes only.

Certain stock imagery © iStock.

Because of the dynamic nature of the Internet, any web addresses or links contained in this book may have changed since publication and may no longer be valid. The views expressed in this work are solely those of the author and do not necessarily reflect the views of the publisher, and the publisher hereby disclaims any responsibility for them.

CONTENTS

DEDICATIONS

I dedicate this set of poems to Sharon and Brittany.

Sharon was my wife, best friend, teammate, and companion. I miss her every day, but I know she is with me in spirit. I believe she made a pact with God to grant me this gift of poetry.

Brittany is a friend who has become like family to me. She was the one who first suggested that I could write poetry. She has been so supportive, encouraging, and uplifting during this 'dark period' in my life. I know I could never thank her enough for her visits, emails, calls, and texts.

INTRODUCTION

These poems were written to help me deal with my grief following the passing of my wife. I have shown them to friends and family and everyone has been very encouraging. Even more so, I have shown them to complete strangers who seemed emotionally moved by them.

The purpose behind the publication of these poems is to help others deal with their grief. At least, it will show others who are grieving that they are not alone.

There are poems that are less dark. There are poems which explore the relationship between grief and love, and the importance of love. There are haikus that I wrote to add emphasis to other poems or to express some other thoughts. I encourage the reader to read the poems from the first to the last, which is also the chronological order they were written. You will see lighter poems, and then, poems that are darker as I went through the grieving process and experienced birthdays, anniversaries, and other events.

These poems were written in a 7 month period which began about 3 months after she died. I believe that these expressions of emotions have helped me come to grips with the changes that I need to make as I continue my own journey. I hope the reader can similarly get a different perspective of their grief, and maybe, find some light beyond the darkness.

ARRIVAL

Grief arrived on the first day of March
For a long-duration stay
It came because of a love so deep
Nothing could make it go away

The love is still there
Although the object is no more
Grief is the pain of loss
But, it could not show love the door

As spring changes into summer
And, summer turns to fall
The love remains eternal
But, grief stays through it all

Sometimes grief relaxes its grip
It feels like a new life
But, it returns as strong as ever
And, I realize how much I still miss my wife

Grief is not eternal
It will fade away one day
But, the love will never ever leave
It is the victor in every way

TIME

Time, when will we ever learn?
How many times I fear
We wish we had
Another hour, day, or year?

Time, why do we think we have so much
When we really have so little?
Sometimes, we're pleasantly surprised
Sometime, life is brittle

Time, why do we take you for granted?
Time, why do we leave undone
Words of encouragement and love
To our daughters and our sons?

Time, why is there never enough?
Time, why do you move so fast?
Time, why do we think
That you will always last?

Time, have we learned nothing of your nature?
Time, why do we assume
That we have another Friday
Or yet, another June?

Time, help us use you wisely
And help us understand
To live life with no regrets
And use you the best that we can

LUCKY

I am a very lucky man
I met a woman named Sharon
She became my beautiful wife
Our marriage was long
It lasted over half my life

I am a very lucky man
Although we had no children
I am not really alone
Nieces and nephews visit a lot
Whom I love like they were my own

I am a very lucky man
Brothers, sisters, and in-laws, too
Give me much needed support
They never fail to provide relief
They never ever fall short

I am a very lucky man
I have friends whom have been loyal for many years
Some not seen for a while
But, they rallied quickly to my side
Calling, visiting, and making me smile

It's hard to believe that all these gifts
Are deserved – I know they're not
They must be part of God's grand plan
God has been very good to me
I am a very lucky man

SELFISH?

I know she is in Heaven
Surrounded by God's unbounded love
I know she's warm and safe there
And as beautiful as a dove

But, I would do anything
To have her back for a while
To see her once again
Especially, that beautiful smile

But, am I being selfish
To wish her away from there?
To wish that she be near me?
To touch her auburn hair?

To hold here in my arms again?
To kiss her once or twice?
For only just a little while
It would be so nice

She is with me now in spirit
That wish was never meant to be
But, when I go to join her
Together we'll spend eternity

ADJUSTMENTS

It is so hard to adjust
To being solo instead of a team
We did everything together
It feels like I'm living a bad dream

We would talk and make plans
We would laugh and eat
We respected each other
She was so sweet

We relied on each other
That much is true
But, now without her
What am I to do?

I've no one with whom to share
The events of everyday life
I can't say 'I got the mail'
To my wonderful, loving wife

I will get used to that fact
It may take a while
To acclimate to being alone
With no one to share a smile

After the grief is lifted
Perhaps one day I will find
Someone with whom I can share
Someone who will treat me in kind

Until then, I will do my best
To do the things to make her proud
I will always love her
That I will say out loud

FORCES

Memories and distractions
Are the opposing forces of grief
Memories bring it on
Distractions provide relief

One day you walk outside
To bring in the mail
Looking at the name on the envelope
You start to cry and wail

Another day you find yourself
Immersed in a pool of tears
Until you hear the phone
And smile at the name that appears

Both forces are needed to balance it out
Grief must run its course
Tears must be shed
Crying until you become hoarse

Without some distractions
Easily you fall into the abyss of despair
Sometimes all it takes
Is a laugh or some fresh air

Both are needed to recover from grief
Remember the love – Allow the tears
Take care of yourself – See your friends
Grief will ease, but it may take years

HEALING

'Time heals all wounds', it is said
Does it include losing a wife?
The grief can be so overwhelming
It changes more than your life

The bed is half-empty
The house is so quiet, too
It is so hard to decide
What I am supposed to do

Living with all the reminders
Make it especially tough
But, trying to move her things
Can be even more rough

A logic-driven person
After such a loss
Will soon find that
Emotions become the boss

Relationships change with the death of a spouse
Many will say
Some become stronger
While others fade away

When there aren't any children
One needs to rely even more
On sisters, brothers, nephews, and nieces
Walking in through my front door

Friends become much more important
Calling and texting make me smile
But something even better is
Getting together for a while

The waves in the ocean of life keep churning
After a wound so deep
One wonders when it will calm
Time only seems to creep

HABITS

After the passing of my wife I find
Old habits are hard to break
Things I do out of habit
Can make my heart ache

Instead of the pronoun 'I'
I keep using the plural 'We'
And each time it happens
I wish it were as it used to be

Out of habit
Her favorite bread I still buy
With each slice that I consume
I remember her beautiful eyes

Some of these habits
I really don't mind
They served a purpose
I seem to find

There are so many things
I will continue to do
For no other reason than
She asked me to

I'll continue to keep these habits
Until I'm a hundred and five
It's worth a little heart ache
To keep her memory alive

HONORING

How do I honor the memory
Of my beloved wife?
I want it to be something
That will last beyond my life

I promise that the changes to the house
Will be as we had said
But the next owner may well say
I need something different instead

The next generations can be given
The tangible assets you had
Over time they can be damaged or lost
And they would feel rather bad

Along with these gifts
We can continue to be
A true role model
For others to see

A role model is one
Who demonstrates traits
That others can absorb
In internalized states

No action is trapped in a vacuum
The ripple effects abound
The traits that we show others
Can truly be passed on down

We can show others how to be kind
We can show others how to love
We can show others how to be determined
We can show others how to rise above

If this is indeed my legacy
I couldn't be more proud
And if these traits are passed on to others
A better mankind will be found

SHARK

Grief is like a shark
Looking for something to eat
It waits under the surface
Ready to attach some meat

The meat that grief seeks
Is never really devoured
It is available for another attack
The attack can last for hours

The attack can some on suddenly
By seeing an on-screen kiss
It can trigger the memory
Of what I've come to miss

Some can be anticipated
The calendar holds the key
When birthdays and anniversaries
Will remind me of the 'we'

The attacks will be less frequent
As time continues on
And I become hardened to the attacks
Until they are nearly gone

Where there is no more food left
A shark will swim away
But, grief doesn't consume its food
It lies in wait for another day

GOODBYE

Saying 'Goodbye' is never easy
When one has nearly reached their end
It is full of angst and tears
For family as well as friends

What if we don't have that chance
To say that final goodnight?
Sometimes fate intervenes
It just doesn't seem right

How many days do we have?
Tomorrow is not guaranteed
But, we have the present
To honor them, indeed

Since we don't always know
That the end is near
How do we live
To avoid those guilty tears?

Treat each visit like
It could be the last
Take your time there
Don't end it too fast

Each moment we have is a gift
So, as you bid adieu
Thank them for being there
Tell them you love them, too

Life can happen suddenly
With good luck or something cruelly unfair
Avoid those tears of regret
By letting them know you care

ACTIVE

Sometimes your spouse will request
That you rub their shoulders and back
You may be tired yourself
But, you want them back on track

You just sat down
To a nice hot meal
They need salt and pepper
And you get it with zeal

You've been out all day
And, want to be home, you see
They say "Let's stop here"
And "here" you will be

To be with them at the doctors
Requires your vacation time
That's not a problem because
Being with them is so sublime

Starting to watch the movie
They say that they feel cold
You get up and give them the cover
The cover you even unfold

When the love is so deep
That no request will perturb
You would do anything for them
Love is an active verb

CHANGE

The more things change
The more they stay the same
Said some Frenchman
I don't remember his name

The saying seems true
Changes we see with family and friends
Additions are joyful
With subtractions, tears will be spent

All our body's cells, science says,
Are renewed every seven years
From the tips of our toes
To the tops of our ears

Our brains continue to connect
Its neurons to each other
So we can remember
All the good times with one another

Our health ebbs and flows
For better or for worse
It can swing like a pendulum
Sometimes it's a curse

The moon has its phases
The tides rise and fall
Change is the only constant
As we live through it all

Our experiences continue to shape us
Or reinforce who we are right now
We are the sum of our decisions
We continue to evolve even now

The pond of our life has ripples
Some changes are easy to shoulder
Others are harder to accept
The pond is hit with a boulder

HAIKU 1

Aware we all are
That love is an active verb
How do we show it?

GRATITUDE

Having gratitude in the midst of grief
Is a difficult task indeed
The grief can close our mind
We feel like we need to concede

Even through grief, we continue
To get more than we deserve
Good wishes, prayers, and visits
From those who just want to serve

We can start each day
While grieving still
With thoughts of thanks
And thoughts of good will

We can think of those
Who go the extra mile
The family and friends
Who always make you smile

As the grief begins to lighten
Those positive thoughts can increase
So many things to be thankful for
Don't let those good thoughts cease

How can we show our gratitude?
How do we pay it back?
What can we do to show others
When grief has slowed its attack?

You may not realize it
But, grief has changed you
You are more aware
Of what others are going through

When grief strikes another
Learn from those who helped you
Repay their kindness, in turn
Do for others what was done for you

LOVE

Love makes us do crazy things
Some people say
It impacts every decision
Every decision, every day

A man named Paul
Wrote a famous letter
He laid out some actions
To help us love better

Love always perseveres and trusts
Love always protects and hopes
Remember these things
When you feel your love is on the ropes

We don't have a survival instinct
When someone we love is involved
You run right into danger
Anything, until it's resolved

Love makes you strive to be better
Love makes you grieve when they grieve
Love makes you sacrifice your goals for another
Love makes you put them above you, indeed

Are these things really so crazy?
How do they so appall?
Maybe something else is more true
Love is the answer, after all

ONE YEAR

I started chemotherapy
Exactly one year ago today
And yet this morning
I ran a 10K

So much change
In a calendar year
We shared many laughs
We shed many tears

My beloved spouse
For a few months has been gone
It's so hard to believe
It's been tough to hang on

But, I have promises
That I need to keep
To keep her memory alive
And taking time to weep

In these few months
There have been many ups and downs
I'm closer to family and friends
I've cried enough tears in which to drown

I've been through radiation and chemo
In the past year of my life
But, the worst part of all
Was losing my wife

As her birthday approaches
I feel even more grief
It's hard to explain
It's hard to get relief

I will continue
To do the best I can
To look outwardly
To continue my plan

I will get through this
I have great support
And doing what I must
I won't fall short

MARCH 1, 2019

Friday, March the first of 2019
Was the worst day of my life
It was the day
God summoned my wonderful wife

The night before she passed away
She had a slight rattle
It wouldn't go away
We didn't know it would be such a battle

Just after midnight on March first
'Happy March' I said with some concern
But, she seemed fine
And wished me a 'Happy March' in return

Later, she kept saying
'OK, OK, OK'
Looking back, I believe
She was asking God to delay

She asked me to call the nurse
After 3 o'clock that morning
She was there quickly
Then, she gave me the warning

The 'death rattle' is what she called it
Not good for my beautiful bride
Pneumonia might be the cause
Looking on the bright side

I texted her nieces and sister
I talked to the one who's a nurse
She asked 'Is this going to take her?'
'Will she get any worse?'

I went to get the prescription
And get us both some food
I didn't think it was that bad
Although I knew it wasn't good

A nebulizer arrived a bit after 10
After that, she looked rather dry
I gave her some water
For her lip balm, upstairs I did fly

After I put the balm on her lips
I believe she said with her smile
'Thank you, I love you, too'
"I'll be alright" and 'Goodbye for a while"

I stepped away for a moment
When I returned to the room
There was no rattling sound
What was I to assume?

"BREATHE, PLEASE BREATHE" – I screamed
In her neck, I saw a heartbeat
She took another breath
Then, God she did meet

I take solace in the fact
That before she left for above
My last act to her
Was an act of comfort and love

And also that she was able
Before leaving me for above
Her last act to me
Was an act of comfort and love

COMPARING

Comparing yourself to others
Is a risky thing to do
It can make you feel unworthy
It can make you envious, too

Sometimes getting the thing
That you have lusted for
Isn't as pleasing as you thought
It becomes a big bore

You've heard the many stories
Of lottery winners going broke
It really does happen
It's not a big joke

When you play the 'if only…' game
In a fantasy land you abide
Your mind is so distracted
In reality, you need to reside

The more you think about what others have
And that's all you're thinking of
You choose envy over gratitude
You choose envy over love

Instead of wishing for
Something else or something more
Maybe you already have what you need
Nothing less, nothing more

When you feel that you are unworthy
Or you're not doing enough
Remember that things do not make you
You are worthy of love

HAIKU 2

Grief is very cruel
Using our love against us
The love is worth it

CAREGIVER

For the caregiver
Death can be a relief
But, that doesn't mean
That there is any less grief

I no longer have to cook her meals
But, I would have
I no longer have to wash her clothes
But, I would have

I no longer have to get her medication
But, I would have
I no longer have to help her get around
But, I would have

I would have done
These things and more
For another hundred years
Because she I adored

Yes, there is relief
Of fewer things I must do
They were so much easier
Than bidding her adieu

MARCH 1, 1980

Saturday, March 1, 1980
Was one of the best days of my life
It was the first day
I spent entirely with my future wife

The day before was 'leap-year day'
For that reason, a party was planned
I invited some work friends over
It wasn't supposed to be very grand

Overnight, the weather turned
We got a real good snow
It looked kind of bad for the party
I hated to cancel, you know

My neighbor below me and I
Had been out on a couple of dates
I asked if she needed supplies
Or if she was willing to wait

I decided to go get groceries
For the party to be held that night
So, she went with me to the store
The drive was a bit of a fright

We made it there and back
The roads were still quire slick
I decided to cancel the gathering
I needed to call people quick

So, the party boiled down
To just her and me
We talked, ate, and watched
Bond with George Lazenby

It was late when she left that evening
As I got myself ready for bed
I kept thinking about her
And dreaming of her in my head

The next morning when I awoke
I knew I wanted to see her more
'Last night was Heavenly'
Said the note she slid under my door

Needless to say, that night
Was a turning point in my life
Only 24 weeks later
We became husband and wife

PROPOSAL

Many men will 'pop the question'
Where the bride would be surprised
However, with my proposal
Both of us were surprised

A trip to Hawaii was scheduled
For some friends from work and me
It would last a week
That was a long time for Sharon and me

The night before we were to leave
In her apartment we were kissing
In a Déjà vu moment
I knew what my life was missing

I dreamt of a beautiful woman
This dream was many years ago
In that moment, I knew that she was the one
From my arms, I couldn't let her go

I had no intent on proposing
When I walked into her place
I knew my love for her had grown
That which nothing could erase

But I said "There's something we ought to consider"
She said "What could that be?"
I said "What about marriage?"
No one was surprised more than me

She recoiled at my question
Her eyes as large as plates
A moment later after it sank in
She smiled starting to deliberate

There's no need to answer right now
In a week I'll be back from my trip
We can get together then
As I continued to kiss her lips

The Friday after I returned
We went out on a date
We went to a Chinese restaurant
We didn't talk about our fate

As we walked out to the car
"Do you want to get married?" I asked
She said "Yes – but only to you"
In our mutual loved, I basked

MIRACLE

A miracle is something
That is exceedingly rare
How many coincidences does it take
To make one or a pair?

In mathematical terms
Something is a rare event
If its probability of occurring
Is less than five percent

All life is very precious
The chances of it existing is small
We are each a miracle
It's amazing we exist at all

The odds were one in 40 million
On the day you were conceived
That you would be 'you'
That's just the DNA that was achieved

Even identical twins
Experience life differently
Even their fingerprints
Are unique, incidentally

We are the consequences of our decisions
We are the sum of our DNA
We are the results of our upbringing
We continue to change every day

We need to look into the soul
And way beyond the physical
Treat everyone with love
Each of us is a miracle

GONE

My wife has been gone
About 6 months today
The grief stays with me
I still cry every day

Her beauty was such
That no one could deny
I miss my best friend
A good reason for which to cry

Cancer was the cause
It would not relent
She fought hard
Then, to Heaven she went

I did all I could
I did all she wanted
I know it wasn't my fault
But, sometimes, I feel haunted

Grief and loneliness
Are a formidable pair
It's hard to imagine
Unless you've been there

I am getting through it
The best that I can
I think I'm doing pretty well
I have a good plan

But, if I could reverse it
I would – whatever the cost
Because the next four words are true
She's gone – I'm lost

TOGETHER

My wife was beautiful
She was also very smart
She had varied interests
Like psychology, law, music, and art

Her psychology degree
Was very useful, I will report
For her classes
I gave her my full support

The paralegal classes
She took much later
They came in handy
Although, she was no litigator

Her art and music
Were longtime loves
She was so good
They fit her like a glove

I always had an interest
In studying the human brain
Psychology was a discipline
That I could easily explain

To the law library
We went as a team
I learned to enjoy it
Like a bowl of ice cream

To museums and concerts
I went with my wife
They were required for her
They added enjoyment to my life

I have always been a sports fan
Watching hockey and basketball
She really learned to appreciate
These sports, after all

She knew the teams in the NHL
And Crosby, Ovechkin, Rinne, and Rask
If you wanted to know more
She, you just needed to ask

My basketball team she came to love
Together we watched every game
If we lost, we were sure
That the referees were to blame

Both of us continued to grow
Day after day, year after year
The other needed to keep up
To avoid those lonely tears

To make a marriage work
You need to do your part
Because either you will grow together
Or you will grow apart

HAIKU 3

Six months since she died
I still wear my wedding ring
Grief overwhelms me

SEARCHING

I had been searching for you
My entire life
I didn't know where to look
To find my future wife

So, God sent you to find me
The apartment below me
He arranged for you
So you, I could see

We met in the parking lot
Both coming home from dates
We had no idea
That God had set our fates

That night when I mentioned
My "Star Trek" collection
I didn't know there would be
Such a future affection

Our first date was spent
With pizza and a movie
I was so lucky
To be seen with such a beauty

We got to know each other
Not by going out
But, by staying in
Our conversations removed all doubt

You could talk about anything
Your intelligence really showed through
I was very moved
I could think about only you

My proposal was a surprise
To me as well as to you
But, when you know they are the one
You do what you have to do

When you said "Yes"
It calmed my nerves
Because having you as my wife
Was more than I deserved

HAIKU 4

Grief and loneliness
Pain and no one to talk to
The pain has doubled

WEDDINGS

From when I was a child
Until just a little while ago
I didn't understand why
At weddings, tears would flow

I thought that happiness
Would put smiles on faces
And not see where
Tears had left their traces

I have seen women sob
And men choke back tears, too
I didn't understand
What they were going through

The bride is so beautiful
And all dressed in white
The groom is looking his best
Everything is just right

As the minister begins the vows
He starts with "To have and to hold"
I used to have a wife
Holding her never got old

The vows continue with
"For richer or poorer"
She enriched my life
Her passing made me much poorer

The next one reads
"In sickness and in health"
This one I know all too well
Having her back would be worth my wealth

The last one goes
"'Til death do us part"
Death was the only way
You could find us apart

Then, they are pronounced man and wife
They are given permission to kiss
It is another reminder
Of what I used to have, but now miss

You now know why I cry at weddings
Whether in person, movie, or TV
It reminds me of our life together
It reminds me of the "we"

HIGHWAY

"Life is what happens
When you were busy making plans"
The quote has never been truer
Fate is not in our hands

Our life is like a highway
Somedays you can go fast
The road is straight and smooth
It seems easy to forecast

But, life is constantly changing
Our decisions can alter the road
Sometimes, it smooths it out
Sometimes, the speed limit has slowed

Health issues can happen quickly
And we have to slam on the brakes
We may have to pull into the emergency lane
You know what might be the stakes

Big decisions like
Marriage, job, or change of abode
Can add some curves, bumps,
Or snow to the road

But, meeting your soulmate at a party
You hadn't planned to attend
Adds hairpin turns and construction zones
With which you'll have to contend

Sometime the final exit
Comes suddenly and with surprise
Family and friends are shocked
At the sudden demise

While others approaching the exit
Their signal has been flashing for years
But, it doesn't follow
That there are any fewer tears

Go ahead and make your plans
And Fate sits back and smiles
You assumed one destination
But, you were off by miles

WRONG

My wife was diagnosed with cancer
About five years ago
Soon, there was chemo
We had to go with the flow

Of course, there were side-effects
She didn't feel real good
She asked me if I thought she'd go
I hoped I had misunderstood

Surgeries were in the plan
She came through them quite well
She started to exercise again
She even bought herself some barbells

Then, the harsh treatments began
But, optimistic was I
I didn't think that it would take her
I didn't think that she would die

Some days while in hospice
She wondered if she would succumb
Again and again, I told her "No"
I had reasons why she would overcome

That last night in March
She said she didn't want to be gone
I told her not to worry
Just keep on keeping on

She asked me another time or two
If I thought that she was gone
I kept saying "No, not now"
Until, sadly, I was wrong

BREAKTHROUGHS

Breakthroughs come in conversations
Which have these three traits
It's the right person, time, and place
That make the idea relate

The right person may tell you
Something you would usually put at bay
But, later you start to think about it
In a totally different way

Sitting in my kitchen
I showed her something I wrote
"You could be a poet"
Was her exact quote

Internally, I dismissed that thought
Poetry was not in the plan
But, the idea stuck with me
The next morning, I said "Maybe, I can"

So, I started the first poem
The lines rolled out of my brain
It was hard to stop crying
I was living in grief's domain

An hour went by
And the poem was complete
Those who read it liked it
I say without conceit

Then, a few days later
I wrote a second and a third
Before this, I thought
That my writing poetry was absurd

It's been three months since I started
Over thirty have been finished
It's hard to imagine life without it
Without poetry, I'd be diminished

All of this happened
And my pen started to sing
Because at the right time and place
The right person said the right thing

THANKS

For more than six months
You've been in Heaven
The grief within me
Still has not lessened

You were my wife
Companion and best friend
You took care of me
Until the bitter end

About six years ago
I wasn't so well
I had drenching night sweats
Not good, you could tell

They found a tumor in my colon
The doctor exclaimed "Wow"
"Your appendix may burst, too"
"Go to the hospital now"

Two days later
I had an operation
I seemed fine
There was much elation

I was discharged from the hospital
Too soon, it turned out
We thought I was fine
But, soon, we had our doubts

You noticed something was wrong
The second morning I was back
I was dehydrated and more
You took action and started to attack

You called the ambulance and doctor
Amazingly, at the same time
I could get dressed or go as I was
The choice, you said, was mine

I got to the hospital
They started an IV
Avoiding a second surgery
Was not meant to be

After the surgery was over
And I returned to the room
I started talking about probabilities
Your smile lifted the gloom

When I returned home
There was much work to be done
But, you were consistently with me
Making sure I had won

You were always there for me
Thank you for saving my life
But, even more importantly
Thank you for being my wife

PRICE

People deal with grief
In many different ways
Some sit quietly and cry
Others smile and say they're OK

Some want to be alone
When dealing with grief
To others, that's absurd
That's no way to get relief

Loneliness can enhance the grief
Because there's no one to talk to
When the house is empty
It is harder to get through

Alone with your memories
Many you don't want to forget
The cycle continues
With a twinge of regret

Phone calls and visits
Help for a bit
But, when they are over
Loneliness returns, you would admit

Even while grieving
This could be fun
You need to make new friends
Or visit some old ones

You have to understand
There is no quick fix for grief
It has stolen your joy
It is nothing but a thief

The stages of grief are
Denial, anger, bargaining with God,
Depression, then acceptance
Taking many years would not be odd

Grief is cruel
Grief is dark
It uses your love
And tries to remove that spark

We pay a price to have loved
And grief is that cost
The love was worth the price
Of having the grief for the one you lost

PIANO

She played the piano
At a store in the mall
When I first heard her play
I knew her talent wasn't small

As I walked closer
I saw no music on the stand
She played with real feeling
It certainly wasn't bland

I thanked her for sharing her talent
"You play beautifully", I said
That was my first meeting with her
I hoped it didn't go to her head

Another day, she played some variations
On Beethoven's 'Fur Elise'
I told her I loved it
And please don't ever cease

Every time I heard her play
I complimented her on her talent
I truly meant what I said
I wasn't just being gallant

The last time I saw her
Beautifully, she continued to play
I told her how much I enjoyed it
I was about to walk away

But, then, she smiled and said to me
"I want to thank you so much"
"For everything you've said"
"I am really, very, very touched"

"Confidence is what you have given me"
"With all your kind words and acts"
Confidence was something
I didn't think she lacked

I was quite moved
At the very thought
About what my few words
To her, they had brought

I was humbled
As tears formed in my eyes
I told her the story
Of my wife who had died

My personal philosophy has changed
Either "Thank you" or "I love you", I always say
"Thank you for sharing your talent"
"And, I love the way that you play"

Whether or not I see her again
I will always deem it absurd
To ever underestimate the power
Of sharing a kind word

DECISIONS

When we make big decisions
We know to expect big effects
But, sometimes, the smaller choices
Can make changes that are complex

When you make a big decision
We take time to do research
We are prepared for all outcomes
We are not left in a lurch

But, choices we make unthinking
Or with no time of spare
May surprise us at the outcome
That those choices we make will bear

A quite extreme example
Is a very tragic tale
A man was killed by a drunk driver
After deciding to get his mail

Deciding to do something illegal
Can be obviously sad
It can have long-lasting effects
You'll wonder what you might have had

Taking an elective in college
You don't know who you'll sit beside
A spark may start to appear there
She might be your future bride

A new coach is coaching your brother
And you decide to go to the game
There, your eyes will meet
Soon, you'll have the same last name

You decide to sit at the counter
You converse with someone sitting near
The conversation steers to a common interest
A new friend has just appeared

Coincidences might be another name
For these small decisions we make
These decisions are part of living
There is always some risk to take

We need to expect the unexpected
As we live from day to day
Which small decision might be the catalyst
That can change your life today?

HAIKU 5

Everything I do
Running, poetry, reno
Is to make her proud

WORDLESS

'I love you'
Is a very important phrase
But, one can say it without speaking
In many different ways

Couples who have been together
For more than a little while
Can say 'I love you'
With just the right smile

Pouring their morning coffee
With the perfect amount of cream
Will say 'I love you'
And make the other beam

Couples holding hands
Or when just pinky fingers touch
Can say loud and clear
'I love you so much'

One enters the room
The other turns their head to meet
Their eyes twinkle at each other
The 'I love you' is unspokenly sweet

The body language can say it
Because it never lies
Just the way one stands or sits
'I love you', it will apprise

The last act to my wife
Was putting balm on her lips
It said 'I love you'
In a way that nothing could eclipse

Her last act to me
Was smiling with those lips
With it 'I love you' was said
Then, to Heaven, she made her trip

Whether alone or in a crowd
There are ways not to be deferred
That can say 'I love you'
Without saying a word

BOOMERANG

When bad things happen
To those who do bad things
The word 'karma' is invoked
And, we hope it really stings

But, what about those
Who try to do what's right
Who try to do what's kind
Who try to do good day and night?

There are consequences
For everything we do
Whether the act is good or bad
They will happen to you

'No good deed goes unpunished'
The humorous saying goes
But, that is not the truth
It's something everyone should know

The punishment is already there
For doing a bad deed
But, for a kind act
There is a reward, indeed

Beyond that moment in time
Those kindnesses can have impacts
It can cause other kind acts to occur
The process give one some payback

The payback is not immediate
You can't time it like a roast
But, it will come at a time
When you need it the most

The boomerang effect
The kindnesses contain
Ends up helping the helper
And, the cycle continues again

MISS?

You asked me if I would miss you
After you were gone
I said "More than you can imagine"
I didn't know how I could go on

It has been so tough
To get over losing you
I've barely scratched the surface
But, I do what I have to do

Work has been a good distraction
Even though I dislike oncall
It adds structure to my day
Although each day, I bawl

Friends have been so supportive
With visits, emails, texts, and calls
There are no words to express the meaning
They have lightened that big black wall

Some of my friends
That I've known longer than you
I hadn't seen for decades
But, they came to my rescue

I've never been closer to family
I depend on them so much
They listen to me and advise
They have come through in the clutch

My running is helping me
To be in the best shape of my life
But, I would give it up in a second
To have you back as my wife

My poetry is a gift
That you asked God to give me
It helps me express my emotions
For my recovery, it is a key

The renovation has begun
It seems to be lifting the clouds
I hope the decisions I've made
Are making you very proud

Yes, I do still miss you
You're absence cause me pain
The grief still stays with me
But, the love will always remain

TRANSFORMATIONS

As rooms can be transformed
By using the right décor
Our lives are transformed
By our experiences even more

We are reinvented
Our personalities continue to change
Something we did when we're younger
We wouldn't do as we age

Our parents are a huge influence
They shape us in so many ways
These lessons are so ingrained
They are hard to break even today

We transform physically
We gain or lose weight
We grow from infancy to adulthood
Even our hair is styled, colored or goes straight

With a new job
New challenges will abound
They will expand your horizons
The changes in you may astound

When moving into your first house
Your priorities are adjusted
Dealing with yard work
And painting things that have rusted

Transformations can take a dark turn
After some very tragic news
One can become paranoid
Or constantly live in the blues

After a loved one passes
Exploring things never tried before
Or embracing a common interest
Can make you appreciate them even more

The loss of a loved one
Can change us in many ways
Grief can be overwhelming
Remember their love is there, always

Most changes are incremental
Very few are really large
Those that are can be rather bad
But, through them, you must charge

These transformations are part of life
We will get thought them in the end
To assure that this is true
You need a good set of friends

Each of these transformations
Plays an important role
In creating your life's tapestry
In part or as a whole

THANKFUL

It's easy to be thankful for
The good things in life
The raise in pay, good health,
Or the marriage with no strife

But, what about the things
Which may cause you pain
Or frustrates, annoys,
Or makes you go insane?

Catching every red light
Driving to the mall
But, had I arrived earlier
I wouldn't have seen my friend at all

The drought this summer
Turned lawns brown and caused farmers pain
I am thankful for it
Because, I didn't have to run in the rain

When I graduated from college
Jobs were hard to find
I went to graduate school
And expanded my mind

My time in graduate school
Changed my life's course
I met such good friends there
And learned so many lessons, of course

Going through my colon cancer
Wasn't a great deal of fun
I learned what to expect
When Sharon was under the gun

When she fought her cancer
I learned some lessons, too
So, I could anticipate
What prostate cancer would put me through

Had my wife not died
My poetry wouldn't have been written
I wouldn't be running either
I would just be sittin'

Good things have happened
After my wife passed away
But, I don't think I can be thankful
For that sad event today

AIRPORT

I was waiting in line
Trying to get an earlier flight
She was just behind me in that line
She wanted to be home by midnight

I had just bought some mints
So, I offered her one
She declined as she was chewing gum
Our conversation had just begun

I mentioned my craving for mints
After eating certain fish
She chewed her gum for a similar effect
And hoped to get her wish

I asked where she was from
She said close to the Football Hall of Fame
I said 'We had been there'
And we were glad we came

We talked about "Friendly's"
And how it is no more
I told her of my 'fruit and dairy' snack
And the combinations I adore

These kinds of conversations
Seem to go all over the place
She said she use to run
I told her about my half-marathon race

It was my turn to see the agent
So, I moved out of the line
I became a standby on the next 2 flights
Everything for me was fine

I went back and told her
That I seemed to be all set
I wisher her luck and I hoped
That she liked what she would get

I took a walk to stretch my legs
And returning, I saw her at her gate
Apparently, that flight was full
Again, she would have to wait

Once again, I wished her luck
And, I reached out my hand
I told her my name was Roy
She said her name was Fran

That was the last time I saw her
But, it is interesting how the meeting went
And, all because I offered her
A small peppermint

GRIEFLESS

If I had a magic wand
Which would eliminate grief
Think of the millions of people
Who could finally get relief

A world without grief
Would seem like a wonderful place
No more crying and sobbing
With tears rolling down our face

Are there other consequences
Of having such a power?
Would it be sweet
Or would it simply sour?

The loss of someone loved
Is grief's root cause
The prospect of which
Is enough to give us pause

If eliminating grief
Means we never love
What would life be like?
Why bother to rise above?

Life without love
Wouldn't be much of a life
We wouldn't be able to love
Our husband or our wife

Our parents and our children
Would not be loved, as well
Without love, we might as well
Be sitting in a prison cell

If eliminating grief
Comes at such a price
I would break the wand in two
And break those pieces twice

Having the love
Is worth the cost
Of the time grieving
For the one you lost

HAIKU 6

A sacrifice is
Giving up something you love
For someone you love

JOY

There are few things as precious
As a child's unadulterated joy
When they are opening a present
Containing a much-wanted toy

The joy is so infectious
It affects everyone around
It puts a smile on their faces
It doesn't matter if they had a frown

Listening to a baby's laugh
Is sure to make you do the same
You wonder why you're not like that
And why you're the person you became

As we grow up, it's harder
To be that joyful once more
Life begins to taint us
It limits the joy we adore

As we get older
The pendulum swings the other way
Life throws us curves
As we live from day to day

I wish there was a way
We could live life like a child
Everything would be new again
The thought alone makes me smile

We learn to be an adult
It certainly has some perks
But, oh to be that child again
All that joy and not have to work

HURRICANE

Hurricanes are said to be
Earth's most powerful storms
They are very important to life
I would humbly inform

The winds of a hurricane
Will spread spores and seeds
From which plants will grow
And on which animals will feed

They break up bacteria
And the dreaded red tide
It adds oxygen to the water
For the fish that reside

Around the globe
They balance heat
Leaving cooler water behind
Slowing others that they greet

We know that hurricanes
Leave behind much destruction
It takes years to recover
And takes lots of construction

The loss of a loved one
Is an emotional hurricane
There may be positive effects
But, the grief causes us pain

We experience no emotion
Stronger than grief or love
When the loved one is taken
Grief is all we can think of

With some losses
It's a category five
You don't know how to go on
With that love deprived

Rebuilding a heart
Will take the time it takes
It would be easier
To predict the next earthquake

But, good things can happen
After the hurricane strikes
You'll see your family members
And your friends that you more than like

You will find that get togethers
Can be very healing
Although, through it all
The grief will keep you reeling

It's hard to get through life
Without experiencing grief
And, the greater the love
The deeper the grief

SACRIFICE

In baseball, a sacrifice
Is making an out
In order to advance a runner
Or bring a run about

In life, we sacrifice
By giving up something we love
In order to help
Someone we love

That something could be money or time
Or time spent in bed
Vacation days from work
Or even your life, I read

Doing something nice for another
Is a sacrifice albeit small
It shows love at a level
That puts them, at that moment, above all

For you, your child sacrifices cartoons
To make you breakfast in bed
You accept the thoughtful sacrifice
Take a bite, and clean up the mess instead

We need to accept the sacrifice from others
Whether large or small
It means they love you
Refusing it would surely appall

Each of us makes a sacrifice
For a loved one every day
And if you think about it
They sacrifice for you in other ways

Sacrifice and love
Are like a hand in glove
Love makes you want to sacrifice
And sacrifice comes from love

TENSE

It's strange that I refer
To her only in the past tense
The grief stays with me
It is still quite intense

There is no more
"We are planning", "She is", or "We're going to"
The verbs are now
"Did", "planned", or "used to"

She was very beautiful
She was quite talented, too
She didn't like math
But, stats and trig, she got through

Thinking about holiday traditions
That we had in the past
It is forever "used to"
"How will I get through?," I ask

If I start a new one
It means I leave her out
When continuing the old
More tears will come about

Maybe tweaking the old
With something brand new
Will keep her spirit alive
And make me not so blue

When I speak in future tense
She can't be a part
But, there's one place she'll always be
And, that's within my heart

KNOWLEDGE

I may be smart
And know lots of things
But there are some topics
Where I don't know anything

I can prove that there are
An infinite number of primes
I can write poems
Which have perfect rhymes

I know the speed of light
In terms of furlongs per fortnight
Did you know you can't sneeze
When you're sleeping at night?

Table sugar's chemical composition
Is no mystery to me
I can make a peanut butter smoothie
As easy as one, two, three

I have made
A tres leche cake from scratch
In softball, I played outfield
And made an amazing catch

In inches, I know
The distance from the Earth to the Moon
From poison ivy
Some people are immune

I can tell you
The atomic weight of gold
I could read
Before I was five years old

I don't know why
God has blessed my like this
But, if I didn't say thanks
I would be very remiss

Another thing that I don't know
I could say for my life
How do I ever recover
From losing my beautiful wife?

MARATHON

Dealing with grief
Is a marathon, not a sprint
It doesn't give you a clue
It doesn't give you a hint

It comes on suddenly
It hangs on tight
It hangs on for months
With no end in sight

There are times
That it decides to tease
It plays hide and seek
And comes back by degrees

I know that grief
Is not a sprint
But, I wish it was
Something that needed a splint

Then, I would know
When the healing was done
And, I could resume life
With the victory won

That's not the way grief works
Grief is very cruel
It knows the love is still there
And uses it for fuel

You'll remember a birthday
Or some other event
And then you'll realize
That you're not over it yet

How will you know when it's over?
How long will you feel these pains?
The deeper the love that was
The longer that grief remains

PROMISE

I promised I would love you
Until death do us part
I have done that in full
And you're still in my heart

If we each have allotted to us
An infinite amount of love to share
We could love everyone infinitely
And still have love to spare

Any fraction of infinity
Is still an infinite number
And when we speak of love
It will certainly not encumber

Is this like being a parent
For another child there is love to share
Without taking away the love
From other children in your care?

So, does this mean I am free
To search for another mate
With whom I can share my life
With whom my grief will abate?

Finding another I can love
Doesn't mean I love you less
That is a sure thing
You don't have to guess

When I promised to love you
Until death did us part
I knew I would love you forever
You'd be forever in my heart

I have fulfilled my promise
I have done what I said I would do
I know I will always love you
No matter what I decide to do

I know you'd want me to be happy
That much I'm certain of
But, am I ready emotionally
To find someone else to love?

Even if finding someone else
Is something you would not impede
Is it something I just want
Or something I really need?

HAIKU 7

Does grief make cowards
Afraid to move on ahead
Embracing the past?

CHAPTERS

Some chapters in our life
We never want to end
There are some chapters
We never want to begin

The book of our life has chapters
Some can be rather small
But, sometimes they are the ones
With more content, after all

Some chapters are so short
Of your life it only covers a day
On that day, the realizations and events
Forever changed you in many ways

Other chapters in your life
Can be very long
Wishing for a long 'Marriage' chapter
Would certainly not be wrong

We can sometimes tell
When a chapter's last page has turned
As circumstances change
Or sad news has been learned

Multiple chapters can be written
It is my belief
All at the same time
Like 'School' and 'Grief'

Our last chapter starts
But, we don't always know when
We may never realize it
Until it reaches the end

The last chapter has started
Some may be told
But, that doesn't mean
That life is on hold

That last chapter
Can still inspire
It can make others
To you still aspire

We should live each day
As if the last page has begun
So others can know
That there's more to be done

IDIOSYNCRASIES

We all have our idiosyncrasies
A personality quirk or two
When summed together
Makes you uniquely you

Although we don't realize it
We all have those little quirks
It takes others to point them out
And you'll think of them as jerks

Sometimes these qualities
They make you so unique
Others will love you for them
Maybe with a little tweak

It could be that those quirks
Were just the things
That made your spouse
Exchange wedding rings

When these traits are displayed
Only your spouse and God
Accept it without judging
And not think it's odd

You're not part of the crowd
It made you stand out
It's part of your personality
It gives it a shout

One of mine is
The tendency to over explain
She would smile and say
"He's doing it again"

She had an infectious laugh
It was super nice
It would have melted my heart
Even it was made of ice

These traits make us who we are
No matter how odd they may be
They're impossible to eliminate
From them you cannot flee

HAIKU 8

Grief is changing me
Embracing the future now
But I am alone

RUNNING

I got on the treadmill
Three or four times a week
About 20 minutes at a crack
It wasn't to get a great physique

I pushed myself
To see how fast I could go
The treadmill is no substitute
For outdoor running, you should know

Even though my wife passed away
I continued to run
She always liked to hear my stats
The moment I was done

I told someone what I was doing
He said – 'Why not run a 10K?'
I hadn't ever considered
Running that far in a day

So, I decided to sign up
For my first 10K race
I only had 12 weeks to prepare
I hoped it didn't end in disgrace

My first run outside
Was only a 2 mile run
I knew I'd have to do more
I knew I had only begun

I would get up early
To run before work
I needed to be consistent
I hoped I didn't look like a jerk

Even on weekends
Believe it or not
I got up at 6 to run
To avoid running when it was hot

My distance gradually increased
I was doing 3 or 4 miles at a time
I was feeling pretty good
My shirts felt like some slime

My distance continued to increased
My app said I ran a 10K
Later, I remembered
It was the anniversary of my first chemo day

I knew if I could run 10K
I certainly could run half that
So, I signed up for the 5K
And hoped I didn't fall flat

Four weeks after the 10K
A half-marathon would be run
I decided to go all in
My real training had begun

I would tell friends
Of my 'short' runs of 5 or 6 miles
They would first look surprised
Then shake their head and smile

The 5K was no problem
The 10K caused some pain
I kept going for the mini
I wanted to finish and not to strain

The day of the mini
Was a crisp fall day
I started out slowly
I didn't want fatigue to get in my way

I finished in under 3 hours
I had met my stated goal
I was very proud of the run
Running helped make me whole

AFTER

I didn't know what to do
After my wife died
It would have been very easy
Just to sit around and cry

I knew I had to think outwardly
And not just stay in and mope
Getting out everyday
Helped me to cope

My radiation treatment
Followed very soon
It forced me to get out
And, to others, be attuned

I was running on the treadmill
But, that didn't seem like enough
I made a goal to run a 10K
I was sure it was going to be rough

I showed a friend some things I wrote
She saw something I didn't see
She thought I could be a poet
I had no idea that could be me

The next day I wrote my first poem
That weekend, I saw a play
I was inspired to write another
More and more inspiration came my way

Meanwhile, I increased my running
While training for the 10K
I thought about a half marathon
I registered for it that day

I also continued my poetry
I had 40 in 4 months or less
I grew to love writing them
You've already figured that out, I guess

The 5K, 10K, and half marathon
Were done, I proudly say
I really enjoyed the running
I might do it again one day

I spent a weekend in Cincinnati
Seeing friends I hadn't seen in years
It was a great experience
I would do it again, I volunteer

All of these things and more
Have helped moderate my sorrow
Moving steadily forward
Continuing the process for more tomorrows

REGRET

Regret comes in two types
One kind appears like a jet
The moment of the act or word
You feel the pangs of regret

Once that act is done
Or that word is said
It can't be forgotten
It stays inside your head

Maybe you were inattentive
When driving your car
Maybe you dropped an 'F-bomb'
And never meant to go that far

The effects of these actions
Can be physical, emotional, or both
You'll promise never to do it again
You would swear a solemn oath

You feel really bad
An apology will be given
It may be accepted
But, you'll never really be forgiven

You'll remember how
You made them feel
You'll also feel bad yourself
No one will fully heal

If you could go back in time
And undo what was done
You'd do it in a second
And pray for no rerun

The other kind may be worse
It can haunt you for years
Things you wish you'd done or said
That can leave you in tears

You'll wonder how
These acts undone or words unsaid
Might have change your life
Had you followed through on that thread

Missing an opportunity to hug
Or a chance to say 'I love you'
May make you wonder
What your life might have turned into

It's not something you lost
But, something you may have gained
The thought stays with you forever
And you will always feel pained

In the parallel universe
Where that act was achieved
You'll wonder if you'd be sad
Or if you'd be relieved

Everyone has experienced
Regret of both kinds
It's part of human nature
It's part of our human minds

So, let all our actions be kind
And, let all our words be tender
Our words and actions have consequences
Let us always remember

Never let a kind word be unspoken
Or a kind act left undone
Maybe your regret count
Can be held to a maximum of none

HAIKU 9

The tens digit changed
Another decade has gone
How did you spend it?

DECOMPRESS

Decompression sickness is the name
For something commonly called the bends
It affects divers who surface too fast
And, can cause them their end

Those who dive too deep
And, stay too long
But, rise too fast
Do it all wrong

The sudden decompression
Causes much pain
Nitrogen bubbles in their joints
May also be in their veins

When you're in love
That is so very deep
And, the loved one dies
You start to weep

The sudden decompression
Of a deep love that was lost
Will cause emotional bends
Unfortunately, that is love's cost

Grief is the common name
For the decompression you feel
It won't go away
And, there is no appeal

The gas bubbles can be related
To the tears coming out of your eyes
The emotional bends are real
I will sadly advise

There may be a formula
To eliminate the bends
Pressure and time
Can make amends

But, there is no such formula
To cause grief to disappear
There is no timetable
It may take years

Divers don't stop diving
Because the bends can occur
We need to continue loving
Don't the opposite infer

Love is necessary
For one to be content
It is something
For which you'll never repent

REGRETLESS

Grief comes to visit
After a loved one dies
It's an elongated stay
Which comes as no surprise

It puts a hole in your heart
That time can only heal
You will find that your joy
Grief will surely steal

You become more emotional
Reminders of them abound
Any little thing
Can the grief compound

Sometimes you cry for no reason
You don't have a clue
It happens so often
You don't know how to get through

You feel it coming on
You try to hold it in
You know that it is useless
And the sobbing begins

The grief is caused
By a love so deep
Grief doesn't go away
Not even in your sleep

Grief's tears and pain
You continue to feel, and yet
The love you had is one thing
That you'll never regret

CONTROL

Control freaks may not like this
But, there are things you can't control
No matter what you say or do
Total control cannot be a goal

You can't control the traffic
Or if it's a cloudy day
You, your spouse, or child can get sick
You can't control what others do, think, or say

Those are facts you can't deny
You need to understand this now
Would you really want to control everything
Even if you could somehow?

The unexpected events
Can bring much joy
They don't happen on a schedule
But, they are things you totally enjoy

Controlling everything means
You will stop or delay
Those surprising gifts of joy
From being on their way

Death and taxes are said to be
The two things you can't halt
Death is undefeated
For taxes, you'd better not default

Trying to control the things you can't
Sounds like a recipe for stress
Instead of putting pressure on yourself
Maybe it's time to reassess

Your emotions are something
That are under your control
Your ability to do that
Can help make you whole

Instead of having a knee-jerk reaction
Take a deep breath and a step back
And consider your words carefully
Before making an attack

Control what you can
Don't try to control the rest
That sounds like a good way
For you to be your best

Not being in control
Lets you see things from another side
You might find that you enjoy
Sometimes being along for the ride

ABOUT THE AUTHOR

This is Roy G. Faulkner's first book of poetry. This book was inspired after the passing of his wife and best friend of over 38 years from cancer.

He is a colon cancer survivor himself who is now battling prostate cancer. That has not held him back from completing his first half marathon in October 2019.

He holds a Master's degree in mathematics from the University of Kentucky. He currently resides in Louisville, Kentucky.

CPSIA information can be obtained
at www.ICGtesting.com
Printed in the USA
BVHW010526290821
615098BV00005B/80

9 781953 397331